Cover & book designed by Paul Tippett and Adrian Andrews for Vitamin P
Picture research by Dave Brolan, Andy Neill and Paul Tippett

ISBN: 9.781.78038.439.9
Order No: OP56386

Exclusive Distributors
Music Sales Limited,
14/15 Berners Street,
London, W1T 3LJ.

Music Sales Corporation
180 Madison Avenue, 24th Floor,
New York,
NY 10016,
USA.

Macmillan Distribution Services
56 Parkwest Drive,
Derrimut, Vic 3030,
Australia.

Printed in China

A catalogue record for this book is available from the British Library.

Visit Omnibus Press on the web at www.omnibuspress.com

KEITH RICHARDS
A life in pictures

OMNIBUS PRESS

London / New York / Paris / Sydney / Copenhagen / Berlin / Madrid / Tokyo

I'm all for a quiet life. I just didn't get one.

KEITH RICHARDS: A LIFE IN WORDS By Andy Neill

"If you're going to kick authority in the teeth, you might as well use two feet."

'The Human Riff', 'Mr Unhealth', 'Keef Riffhard', 'the cat with five strings and nine lives' are just some of the epithets his legend has attracted. "When Keith Richards walks into the room, rock and roll walks in with him" is another hyperbolic attempt to define his Byronic charisma. And certainly it's hard to think of another white English rock 'n' roller, with the possible exception of John Lennon, who commands such genuine and awestruck genuflection. His vampiric look and devil-may-care attitude has inspired a legion of wannabe imitators – New York Dolls, Aerosmith, Guns N' Roses. Black Crowes and Primal Scream to name but several of the guilty. Iggy Pop, no slouch in the rock 'n' roll decadence sweepstakes himself, dedicated his 1982 autobiography *I Need More* to "Keith Richards, my all-time hero".

Despite numerous near scrapes with the Grim Reaper, a unique metabolism, the constitution of an ox and being an important component of the one of the most feted – some would say, pampered – and rewarded group of modern popular entertainers has held him in good stead. No matter how low the gutter, Keith always felt slightly above it. As he pithily commented, "I'd rather be a legend than a dead legend." Richards recently watched his 70th birthday pass in the rear view mirror but clearly has no intention of checking out just yet. As he likes to point out to the hundreds

of thousands who still pack stadiums and arenas worldwide to witness the, quote unquote, Greatest Rock and Roll Band In the World, "Really good to be here… really good to be anywhere!"

There's some kind of supreme irony that a man who oozes Americana should be born in Dartford, an unassuming satellite of London. His maternal grandfather Augustus 'Gus' Theodore Dupree nurtured Keith's interest in music in general and the guitar in particular. "Music is a language that doesn't speak in particular words," Keith stated. "It speaks in emotions, and if it's in the bones, it's in the bones." By the time he had entered Sidcup Art College, after being expelled from Dartford Tech for truancy, he was dashing off Chuck Berry riffs, note-for-note. The life-changing re-emergence of Mick Jagger in his life on a Dartford railway platform in 1961 put them both on a five decades plus course that seems scarcely imaginable in its various twists and turns.

While most bands have a designated lead and rhythm guitarist, The Rolling Stones were unique in that both guitar players swapped roles – sometimes in the course of a song or performance. This "ancient art of weaving", as Richards is wont to describe it, was first perfected in the dank filth of the Chelsea flat that he, Mick and Brian Jones shared in 1962-63. Even at this early stage the differences between Jagger and

Richards were evident – while Mick adhered to his studies at the London School of Economics, Keith (with Brian) shut off the outside world, living on cadged food and the deposits from stolen beer bottles, perfecting the dual guitar sound, learned from their cherished Chicago blues recordings, that helped give the Stones that distinctive edge. "At the time we started none of us were concerned with making it," Keith declared, "we were dedicated to furthering and making known this music we absolutely loved. All we wanted to do was play – with luck, break even – and have some regular gigs. That's as far as our ambition went. Success never came into it. We never dreamed of it, never even thought we could turn the whole of London on to what we were doing, let alone the rest of the world."

Look at sixties vintage footage of the Stones on stage and its Keith who is bandleader – constantly winding and unwinding his body, as the others follow him. His early licks also marked him out among the British beat boom brigade – the savage choppy passages in the remodelling of Buddy Holly's 'Not Fade Away' and the Berry-esque jangle and sharp rolling solo in 'It's All Over Now'. If many (including Jones himself) saw Brian Jones as the leader of the band, Mick and Keith's development as songwriters subtly eroded away that notion. "For some reason Keith and I wrote together," Jagger said in 1979, "maybe because we

knew each other for so long and we're friends. I had no experience to back it with as far as songwriting was concerned. Brian was a much better musician. But it seemed very natural and Keith and I seemed quite good at it. Brian was quite problematical and it was obvious to Keith and myself after trying it a few times that it was going to work. Brian got annoyed but anyone gets annoyed when you exclude them because they're not compatible. I had a slight talent for wording, and Keith always had a lot of talent for melody from the beginning. Everything (in the beginning), including the riffs, came from Keith. But we worked hard at it. We developed it. You need application."

By 1965, with the self-confidence that came from taking a slow Delta blues like 'Little Red Rooster' to number one, Mick and Keith were now able to hold their own, songwriting wise, with singles like 'The Last Time' and 'Satisfaction', the latter fashioned from a riff that was all Keith's, even though he envisaged it for a Stax-like horn section. Keith's acoustic work should not be overlooked – a scene in the 1965 Irish tour film *Charlie Is My Darling* where he picks out a folky tune is a good example of his tasteful feel. Starting with *Aftermath* (1966) his rich, deep chords and picking can be heard to good effect on tracks like 'Mothers Little Helper', 'High And Dry' and 'Take It Or Leave It'.

In 1968, while the Stones were off the road, Keith rediscovered the five-string open tuning used on some of his favourite old blues records, which was to prove a revelation. It also coincided with the Stones "second wind" as Richards described it, commencing with the seminal 'Jumpin' Jack Flash' – the distinctive riff played in open D or open E; live in open G – and *Beggars Banquet*. With Brian Jones' inexorable disintegration, Keith was covering most if not all of the guitar parts himself including slide on 'Jigsaw Puzzle', 'Salt Of The Earth' and 'You Got The Silver' (from *Let It Bleed*). The latter song was also Keith's first fully solo vocal on a Stones track. The open-G tuning became Keith's trademark and was effectively used on such Stones classics as 'Street Fighting Man', 'Honky Tonk Women', 'Gimme Shelter', 'Brown Sugar' and 'Start Me Up'.

In 1969, the Stones were back on the road again – significantly in America, not only the home of the music that inspired them but also where the new rock audience was bigger in numbers and potential lucre. As can be seen in *Gimme Shelter*, the Maysles' important document of that memorable tour, Jagger's persona was shaping into

that of the arrogant rock Nijinsky, while Keith cultivated his unkempt punk gypsy vagabond look. Ironically, glimpsed in "a blink and you'll miss him" audience shot in the Madison Square Garden footage is one John Genzale, a few short years from emerging as the ultimate Richards disciple Johnny Thunders in New York Dolls. Nick Kent, one of the new breed of rock critics at *New Musical Express*, also fanned the flames of the impressionable Keef kult with his on-the-spot Richards' encounters and interviews, not to mention adopting the Stone's sartorial style and nasty habits. "I thought he was just like Lee Marvin in *The Commancheros*," Kent wrote in his book *The Dark Stuff*, "only with better hair and a bad-ass pirate earring, too."

Kent admits that in retrospect he, like many others, found the tales of Richards' wanton behaviour detracted from the bigger picture of the effect the drugs were having on Richards the musician. For a man who had co-written, crafted and played on some of rock 'n' roll's most influential recordings, his achievements and continuing creativity were in danger of being overshadowed by his danger and

drug-fuelled exploits. Indeed, some critics attribute the blame for the Stones' diminishing returns on record from the mid-Seventies onward to Richards' personal problems.

Keith later rationalised becoming an addict as a means of shielding himself from the unreality surrounding celebrity, as he explained in 1992: "Believing your fame is very dangerous. It's not very good for people around you, and even worse for yourself. That's my experience of it. It's one of the reasons I don't regret zooming into the dope thing for so long.

It was an experiment that went on too long, but in a way that kept my feet on the street when I could have just become some brat-ass, rich rock and roll superstar bullshit, and done myself in in another way. In a way I almost see it as I almost forced myself into that in order to counterbalance this superstar shit that was going on around [the Stones]… In retrospect, it shouldn't have worked, but that's what I had to do. When I look at it now, that was one of my rationalisations for it. And the other is, hell, I was just sort of into De Quincey's *Opium Eaters* a century too late. I just saw

myself as a laboratory: '*Well, let's see what this does…*'"

Richards' subconsciously projected image of seventies rock 'n' roll decadence and his exploits, usually with the equally exotic Anita Pallenburg by his side – whether it was bringing a puppy on board a domestic flight against regulations during a UK tour in 1971, his hair-raising encounters with the French police on the Cote d'Azur, or his numerous scrapes with drugs and policemen – were all grist to the mill, reinforcing Richards' raucous reputation. While stories and interviews throughout the period only consolidated this picture it was former Stones confidante 'Spanish' Tony Sanchez's lurid memoir *Up And Down With The Rolling Stones*, published in 1979, that sealed the image for eternity. By the time readers were lapping up Sanchez's sensationalised stories, Keith had cleaned his act up, albeit swapping one vice for another – an Olympian consumption of bourbon and vodka, with cocaine and ganga thrown into the mix. The image of the kohl-eyed junkie gypsy was replaced by the trilby hatted slurring soak – a rock 'n' roll Peter O'Toole from *Jeffrey Bernard Is Unwell*.

The eighties marked a low point in Richards' relationship with Mick Jagger when Mick decided to cut loose for a solo career that failed to match expectations. For Keith, it felt like the ultimate betrayal. While Jagger preferred to keep the Stones' dirty laundry from the public, Keith was happy to wave it in front of their noses. "In Paris, I live around the corner from the English bookshop," he said in 1988, "and there was this book in there and in great gold letters it said Brenda Jagger. So he became Brenda for a bit. That was at the time when he was spending more time doing his solo stuff instead of [working with the Stones] which really pissed me off… I very nearly stiffed him at the time. But there's no joy in punching a wimp. I like him, and I say these things, and they come out and they sound kind of cruel but I've known Mick since I was four years old. And despite myself, I do love the guy."

The pair had a rapprochement in 1989 for the recording and writing of *Steel Wheels*, released to coincide with a gigantic American tour which cynical commentators cited as the real reason why the 'Glimmer Twins' kissed and made up. Certainly the two men's working relationship has never recovered its equilibrium but this can be traced further back to 1971 when the Stones left England to become tax exiles and were no longer within easy distance to collaborate. It was also the year when, much to Keith's distaste, Mick began climbing the social ranks by marrying Nicaraguan socialite Bianca Pérez-Mora Macias. "Why have Mick and I stayed together all this time?" Richards pondered in 1991. "Well, we do so somewhat reluctantly. It's when we stop working that Mick and I start sniping and bickering at each other. There are hundreds of things that Mick and I vehemently disagree upon, but the minute we start working again… If we sit down in a room together with just a keyboard and guitar, all that stuff suddenly becomes totally irrelevant."

Other outside projects have helped occupy Keith's time while his beloved Stones take enforced vacations. These include his recording and touring band The X-Pensive Winos, an album of Jamaican Rasta chants with The Wingless Angels plus guest appearances on recordings by friends and heroes such as Tom Waits, Aretha Franklin, Chuck Berry, John Lee Hooker, Buddy Guy, Scotty Moore, Jerry Lee Lewis and tributes to departed friends like Gram Parsons.

Above and beyond the Keith legend endured and accidents happened – a guitar string cutting his finger causing it to be infected, falling off a chair at his home library and most seriously of all in Fiji in 2006, a near fatal skull fracture resulting from a tree fall necessitating emergency brain surgery in Auckland, New Zealand. Doctors warned him that blow was now definitely off the menu. Still Keith couldn't resist one last snort – a fragment of his beloved father Bert's ashes, a story initially misreported to stand alongside the legend of Keith's visit to a Swiss clinic for a blood change. Richards eventually set the record straight in his 2010 autobiography *Life*. "The truth of the matter is that after having Dad's ashes in a black box for six years, because I really couldn't bring myself to scatter him to the winds, I finally planted a sturdy English oak to spread him around. And as I took the lid off of the box, a fine spray of his ashes blew out on to the table. I couldn't just brush him off so I wiped my finger over it and snorted the residue. Ashes to ashes, father to son. He is now growing oak trees and would love me for it."

Thanks to his public image, Richards has been alternately pilloried and parodied in the media. *Daily Mail* journalist Peter Hitchens described him in 2010 as "a capering streak of living gristle who ought to be exhibited as a warning to the young of what drugs can do to you even if you're lucky enough not to choke on your own vomit." In the BBC comedy series *Stella Street*, whose surreal character depictions included Mick and Keith running a corner shop in leafy Surbiton, John Sessions played the guitarist as an incoherent Jack Daniels-swilling, slurring wreck. The ultimate Keith stereotype was portrayed by his actor friend Johnny Depp as Captain Jack Sparrow in Disney's *Pirates Of The Caribbean* series. "It was very strange initially you know when the character's main ingredients came up," Depp told nme.com. "I was a little worried at what Keith was gonna think… Because for a good portion of the time I was spending with him, I was sponging as much of him as I possibly could for the character. And when he found out what I'd been doing, it could've gone either way, but he was very nice about it, like 'I had no idea mate!' He was very sweet about it."

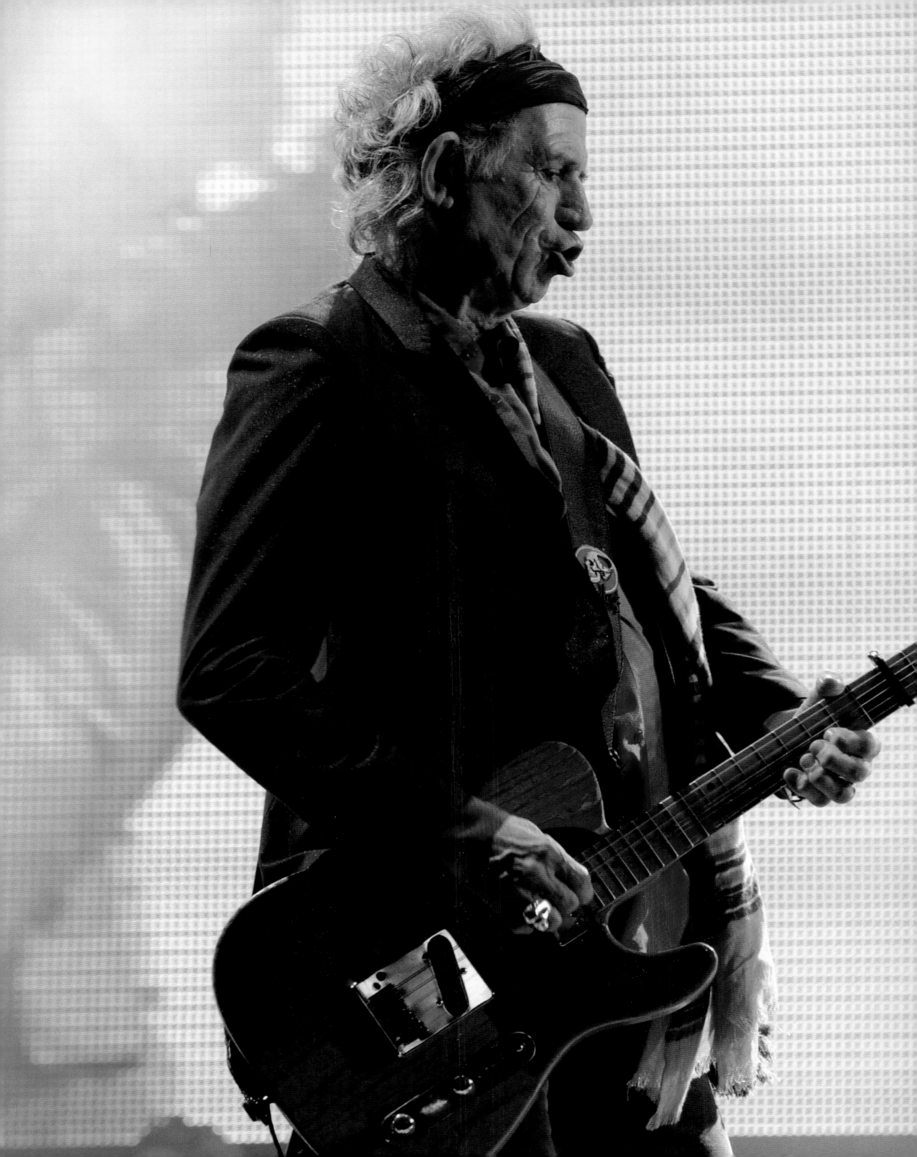

If the adage that most musicians say all they have to say through their songs is largely correct, Keith remains that rare exception of the quotable rock star. While many of his contemporaries regarded the interview as the psychiatrists couch or as a means to bemoan their lot, Richards' published conversations reveal a man comfortable in his own skin; alternately amusing and endearing, combative and opinionated, but frank and forthright, not to mention perspicacious and after five decades, obviously still in love with writing and performing, and ever so slightly bemused that he's around to talk about it. "I don't think that rock 'n' roll songwriters should worry about Art. I don't think it comes into it. A lot of it is just craft anyway, especially after doing it for a long time… As far as I'm concerned, Art is just short for Arthur."

Guitarist, singer, songwriter, author, actor, lover, hedonist, jailbird, father, grandfather – Keith Richards has lived the life and continues to embody the spirit of wilful non-conformism,

although there are those that know a different model. "Keith is very much a friend," says Charlie Watts. "If you are with Keith you are with him for life. He is very honourable like that and very

close. We don't say much, we just look at each other… He is a very quiet guy actually, very quiet. He is nothing like his image."

Let Keith himself have the last word: "There is an image projected that people come for and take away with them and give to their readers if they're journalists, and

obviously there's a lot of me in that image. I've never tried consciously to project it, but there's not really much you can do about it. It's like a little shadow person that you live with. In some

situations, I'll realize, *Uh, no, these people expect me to do a REAL Keith Richards…* and sometimes it's quite funny… As long as you're aware of it, it's something to play with. I'd only get worried if I really became like Keith Richards… whoever HE is."

THE EARLY DAYS – 1963

When they were six… formed in 1962 when pianist Ian 'Stu' Stewart (holding maracas in these pics) answered an ad placed by Brian Jones in *Jazz News*, The Rollin' Stones originally featured 'Mike' Jagger on vocals/harmonica, Keith Richards (guitar), Brian Jones (guitar/harmonica), Dick Taylor (bass) and Tony Chapman (drums). Taylor left to continue his art studies and was replaced by Chapman's mate, William Perks (aka Bill Wyman) and in early 1963, after some persuading, jazz enthusiast Charlie Watts joined up.

THE FAMOUS FIVE

With the arrival of 19-year-old publicist Andrew Loog Oldham as the Stones' manager, the image conscious whiz kid deemed six was too many and so Ian Stewart was relegated to being the unseen, but invaluable, 'sixth Stone' – fulfilling the role of road manager as well as joining the band on stage to play boogie woogie piano on later tours. This photo session from May 4, 1963, the Stones' first, shows the group near the Chelsea Embankment, very close to 102 Edith Grove, the flat that Mick, Keith and Brian shared that was something of a monument to communal squalor.

KEITH RICHARDS, 1963 MODEL

At this early juncture in the Stones' career, Keith was quiet and very much in the shadows cast by Brian and Mick. However, even then, he was the heart of the band's engine room. Bill Wyman: "Something happens when we play together. It's impossible to copy. Every band follows the drummer. We don't follow Charlie. Charlie follows Keith. So the drums are very slightly behind Keith. It's only fractional. Seconds. Minuscule. And I tend to play ahead. It's got a sort of wobble. It's dangerous because it can fall apart at any minute."

TIN PAN ALLEY

The Rolling Stones face Terry O'Neill's camera along Denmark Street, London's Tin Pan Alley, in early 1964. Along with The Beatles, the Stones' were the forces that ultimately helped to dispense with the tried and trusted Tin Pan Alley practice of hawking the right song for an artiste to record. Following the Beatles' example, Jagger and Richards (or 'Richard' as Andrew Oldham had shortened his name) tentatively began writing their own. Denmark Street is also notable for being the location of Regent Sound Studio where, in 1964, the band cut their third single (and breakthrough hit) 'Not Fade Away' as well as their first album. "We did [the album] on a two-track Revox in a room insulated with egg cartons at Regent Sound. Under those primitive conditions it was easy to make that kind of sound but hard to make a much better one."

LOCK UP YOUR DAUGHTERS

The Stones stroll down James Street in Covent Garden with manager Andrew Oldham standing in their shadow (back left). Oldham was instrumental in selling the Stones' unkempt bohemian image as a natural antidote to the Beatles' Establishment-approved mop-tops.

"Things happened incredibly fast from the moment Andrew turned up," Keith wrote in his memoir *Life* (2010). "To me at least, there was a certain feeling that things were running away from us… [Andrew and I] were of a very similar mind – let's figure out how to use Fleet Street."

TIME IS ON MY SIDE

Keith takes a post-meal pit stop, 1964. The pace was gruelling – in that year alone, the Stones played over 300 shows around Britain, Europe and the United States, as Richards remembered. "We worked our asses off from '63 to '66, right through those three years, non-stop. I believe we had two weeks off. That's nothing, I mean I tell that to BB King and he'll say, 'I've been doing it for years'."

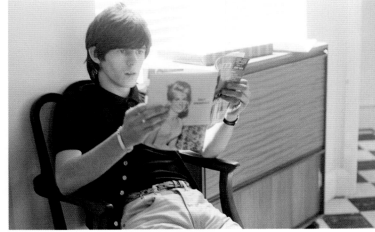

SHARP DRESSED MAN

Keith kicks back during the Stones' first American tour, June 1964. A visit to Hollywood's Beau Gentry menswear store provided the opportunity for a new suit. The band's appearance on *Hollywood Palace* the previous day was less pleasurable where they had to run the gauntlet of host Dean Martin's on-air insults: "Rolling Stones… aren't they great?" (Martin rolls eyes) "They're going to leave right after the show for London. They are challenging The Beatles to a hair pulling contest… Well I'm going to let you in on something… you know these singing groups today… you're under the impression they have long hair. Not true at all… it's an optical illusion… they just have a low foreheads and high eyebrows."

READY, STEADY, GO!

Keith has a vamp on Brian Jones' custom-made Vox teardrop guitar on the set of *Ready, Steady, Go!*, June 26, 1964. *RSG!* was the most important and influential music television programme to ever hit British TV screens. The show "discovered" the Stones in August 1963 and for the next three years, the band and manager Andrew Oldham were frequent guests – on September 10, 1965, they took over a whole episode which was sub-titled 'Ready, Steady, Stones'.

COMING DOWN AGAIN

Keith goes off the rails in Paris, October 1964. The Stones had an even greater following on the Continent than The Beatles and, in later years, would spend much time in the City of Light recording albums such as *Some Girls* and *Undercover* at EMI's Pathe-Marconi Studios, as well as rehearsing for European tours. Both Mick and Keith kept apartments there.

Women are a beautiful complication, and I look forward to far more beauties and far more complications.

WELCOME TO AMERICA

By the time the Stones arrived in New York on October 28, 1965, for their fourth tour of North America and Canada, they were in a comfortable position. '(I Can't Get No) Satisfaction' had reached number one on both sides of the Atlantic and their latest single, 'Get Off Of My Cloud' was about to repeat the feat. "'Get Off Of My Cloud' was basically a response to people knocking on our door asking us for the follow-up to 'Satisfaction'… We thought, 'At last. We can sit back and maybe think about events'. Suddenly there's the knock at the door and of course what came out of that was 'Get Off Of My Cloud'."

BACKSTAGE

Tuning up in dressing rooms backstage on the late 1965 American tour. The band rarely had time to rehearse in those days and soundchecks were non-existent. Any such luxury was academic anyway as the band's brief 30-minute spot would be drowned by a deluge of female screaming from start to finish. "You know that weird sound that thousands of chicks make when they're really lettin' it go? They couldn't hear the music. We couldn't hear ourselves for years. Monitors were unheard of. It was impossible to play as a band on stage, and we forgot all about it."

LIVE IN THE USA 1965

The Stones onstage during the same tour. Throughout his life Keith has had many close shaves; not least when playing Sacramento's Memorial Auditorium on December 3. When trying to move the microphone stand with the neck of his guitar, a blue flash from the ungrounded mike sent Keith flying backwards, knocking him unconscious. The show was stopped, the curtain pulled and he was rushed to a hospital emergency room. It was claimed the thick soles on his suede Hush Puppy shoes was what saved him from a date with his maker. In 2010, while promoting his memoir *Life*, Richards later sardonically commented "my most spectacular moment was in Sacramento."

I'm Sagittarius.
Half-man,
half-horse, with a
license to shit
in the street.

COWBOY KEITH

After the last date on the tour at Los Angeles' Sports Arena on December 5, the Stones had a break before scheduled recording sessions. Keith, Ian Stewart (sitting on bench next to Richards), Ronnie Schneider (the nephew of the Stones' business manager Allen Klein who was working on the tour) and photographer Gered Mankowitz flew to Phoenix for a horse-riding trip into the McDowell Mountains. Having idolised Roy Rogers as a kid, being kitted out in the outfit with guns was the ultimate fulfillment of Keith's cowboy fantasies.

LA LA LAND

Keith at RCA Studios, Los Angeles during sessions for what would become the *Aftermath* album – the first where all tracks were written by the Jagger-Richards partnership.

Sometimes
I think songwriting
is about tightening
the heartstrings as
much as possible
without bringing
on a heart attack.

REDLANDS, SUSSEX

By 1966, the fruits of the previous three years hard graft started rolling in. During the early part of the year, Keith purchased Redlands, a thatched cottage encircled by a moat in West Wittering, near Chichester, Sussex, for £17, 750 via local auction. Quite what the staid residents of Chichester made of this long-haired reprobate moving among them remains unrecorded but, despite the house being the scene of many a drama, Keith still owns the property to this day. When Gered Mankowitz paid a summer visit, his pictures show Keith around the grounds, rowing in the moat and playing with his dog Ratbag. At the same time as acquiring Redlands, Keith bought a blue Bentley, even though he didn't hold a driver's license.

SOME GIRLS

Keith and female admirers at London Airport, June 23, 1966. He and the rest of the Stones were departing for their fifth American tour. "I was 19 when it started to take off, right? And just a very ordinary guy. Chucked out of night clubs, birds poke their tongues out at me, that kind of scene. And then suddenly, Adonis! And, you know, it's so ridiculous, so totally insane. It makes you very cynical."

FEEL ON BABY

The Stones with sister fans Kathryn and Judy Brennan outside the Midland Hotel, Manchester, September 28, 1966. The band were four dates into their autumn tour of the UK – their first British concert appearances in a year. Keith wondered what the Stones' reception would be like now that new teenybop heroes like The Walker Brothers and Small Faces were ruling the roost but he needn't have worried – the reaction was predictably frenzied.

A LOTTA BOTTLE

Mick and Keith strike a pose for photographer Michael Cooper against an advertising hoarding close to Olympic Sound Studios. Starting with recording sessions for *Between The Buttons* in late 1966, Olympic became the Stones' preferred studio, mainly because it was recommended by their valued engineer Glyn Johns who used it as his working base.

COOL, CALM & COLLECTED

Keith at work in Olympic Studios during late 1966-early 1967, photographed by Gered Mankowitz. Like The Beatles, the Stones preferred to record through the night and it was at the end of one such session at Olympic that Mankowitz took the band up to Primrose Hill to shoot the iconic cover image for *Between The Buttons* in the dawn mist (opposite).

BUSTED

The weekend of February 11-12, 1967, when an informal party at Keith's Redlands retreat became the target of a drugs bust, will forever be notorious in Stones folklore. Driving down from London were Keith, Mick, Marianne Faithfull and their friends Michael Cooper, Christopher Gibbs, Robert Fraser, Fraser's manservant Mohammed and mysterious hanger-on David

Schneiderman (known to the hip Swinging London scene as 'Acid King') who vanished shortly after the raid, widely suspected of tipping off the authorities. The weekend had passed uneventfully up to that point with all having ingested LSD and tripping around the Sussex countryside near Redlands as Cooper's pictures convey.

ROUGH JUSTICE

When the case finally came to trial in the last week of June, the world's eyes were on the small town of Chichester where Mick, Keith and Robert Fraser's charges were dealt with separately. Despite the flimsy nature of the prosecution's case, Mick was found guilty of possession of four pep pills without prescription and on June 29 he was sentenced to three months; Fraser received six months for heroin possession and Keith a year for allowing his premises to be used for cannabis smoking. An appeal was lodged and Jagger and Richards were released the following day. Their appeal bid was ultimately successful but Fraser was less lucky and served out his sentence. As details of the case became a matter of public record, Keith's reputation was enhanced thanks to an infamous exchange that occurred between the prosecution and the guitarist when questioned as to the uninhibited state of 'Miss X' (alias Marianne Faithfull) at the time of the police swoop. "We are not old men," Keith informed his interrogator. "We are not worried about petty morals."

These pictures were taken at both ends of the court process; top left at Redlands and enroute to Chichester Magistrates Court where the pair first entered a 'Not Guilty' plea on May 10 and opposite after being released from prison on June 30, meeting the press in The Feathers pub near their counsel's office in the Temple area of London.

HAIR RAISING
Psychedelic Keith and his turned-on hair dryer.

THE ROCK STAR AND THE MODEL

Keith and his new girlfriend, model/actress Anita Pallenberg outside the Excelsior Hotel, Lido, Venice, 1967. Anita was in Italy to film her scenes in Roger Vadim's *Barbarella*. The couple's union was not exactly smooth – Anita was previously Brian Jones' girlfriend but after a stressful excursion to Morocco earlier in the year, she ended up with Keith. Anita exerted a strong presence within the Stones' circle and her taking up with Keith shifted any last vestige of power permanently away from Jones to Jagger and Richards. Under her encouragement, Keith also started experimenting with his look, teasing his hair into its tousled unkempt state and wearing more flamboyant clothing. Keith was metamorphosing into 'Keef'.

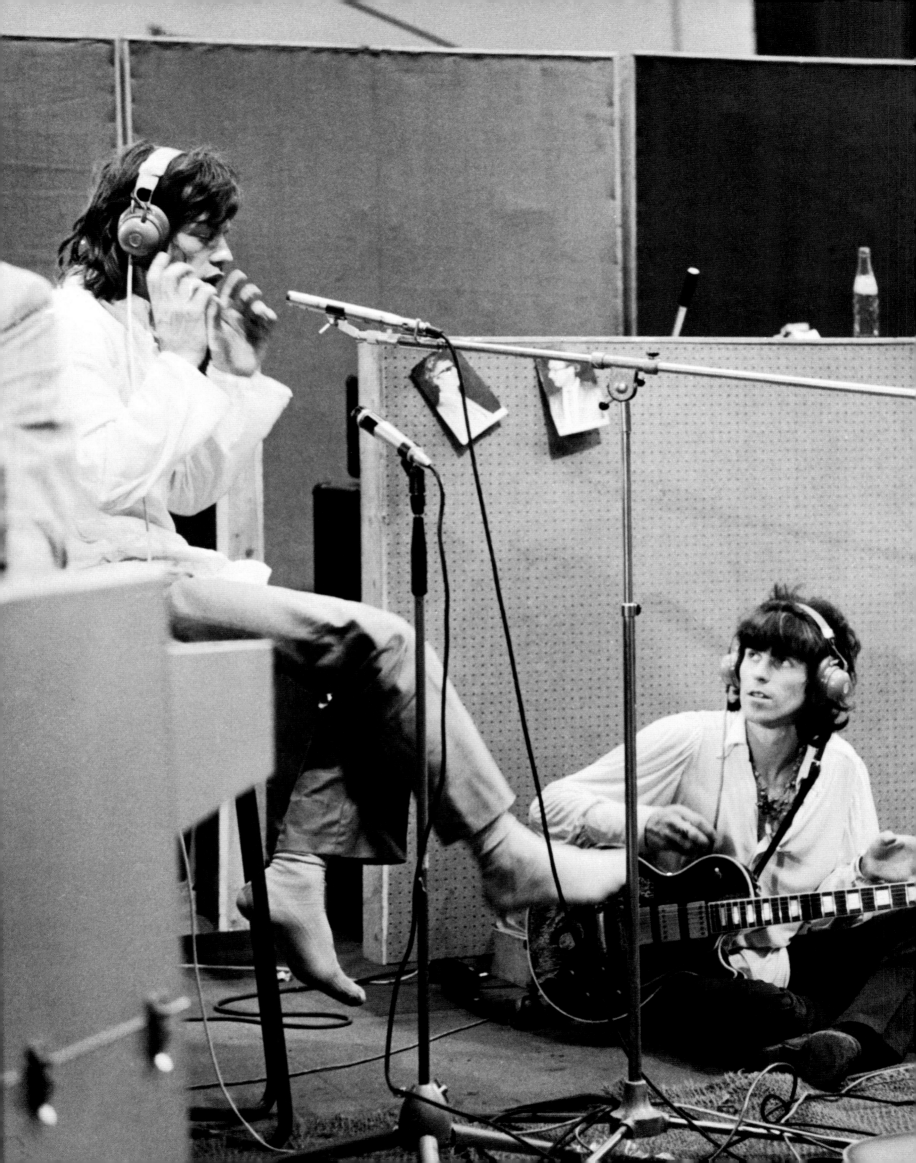

ONE PLUS ONE

Olympic Sound Studios while making
Jean Luc Godard's semi documentary
movie *One Plus One* aka *Sympathy For
The Devil*, June 1968

BIG CHIEF RICHARDS

Keith becomes one with nature in the Mojave Desert during the summer of 1968, photographed by Michael Cooper. He and Anita with friend Gram Parsons (then of The Byrds) went out to the Joshua Tree National Park while Mick and Keith were in Los Angeles mixing the *Beggars' Banquet* album. Parsons' country influence would be felt on tracks over the following Stones albums *Let It Bleed*, *Sticky Fingers* and, especially, *Exile On Main Street*.

ROLL AND STONES

Mick rolls while Brian and Keith strum. "As far as I know Brian Jones never wrote a single finished song in his life; he wrote bits and pieces but he never presented them to us. No doubt he spent hours, weeks, working on things, but his paranoia was so great he could never bring himself to present it to us."

THE ROLLING STONES, MK II

On June 13, the band gathered for a press call at the bandstand in Hyde Park to introduce Brian Jones' replacement, Mick Taylor, and to announce plans for a free live show in the park, the Stones' first proper live concert in over two years. By the time the day arrived (July 5), the event had become a tribute to Brian who drowned in mysterious circumstances at his Sussex home two nights before. The effects of being off the road were evident with the Stones noticeably rusty in parts and the outdoor weather creating tuning problems. Keith and the band used the nearby Londonderry House Hotel as their base of operations before being driven to the park in a converted army ambulance.

PRODIGAL SON

Keith and Anita meet the press on August 18, 1969 – eight days after the birth of their son Marlon at King's College Hospital in Dulwich, south east London. If Keith is to be believed, thanks to his parents' nomadic lifestyle, the first words Marlon learned to say were "room service".

ISLE OF WIGHT 1969

Two weeks later, Keith and Charlie with Robert Fraser (left) and other Stones associates were at the second Isle of Wight Pop Festival to see Bob Dylan perform on August 31. Speaking of an occasion when the two met in a London club in 1966, Keith recalled, "I remember Bob saying to me, 'I could have written 'Satisfaction', Keith, but you couldn't have written 'Desolation Row'.' I said, 'Well, you're right there, Bob!'"

DEAD CERT

Keith in repose during preparations for the Stones' late 1969 American tour. Rehearsals were held on the Warner Brothers soundstage for the film *They Shoot Horses, Don't They?* about a Depression-era dance marathon hence the stakes-betting background prop.

ONSTAGE

Keith in excelsis, back on the boards at Madison Square Garden, NYC, November 1969. The Stones played two nights at the prestigious venue towards the end of their three-week tour, with the debacle of the Altamont free festival in California being added to counter criticism that the Stones were receiving over lateness and high ticket prices. It was on this North American tour that the label "the greatest rock 'n' roll band in the world" was first used by tour MC Sam Cutler when introducing the Stones – a tag that stuck. The seventies were around the corner and the 1969 US trek – which grossed nearly two million dollars – was the blueprint for the vast touring juggernauts the Stones would subsequently undertake.

Fashion thinks more about me than I think about it. I just wore what I wore and people noticed.

DENMARK

Keith playing his translucent plexiglass Dan Armstrong guitar during soundcheck at the Forum, Copenhagen, Denmark, September 12, 1970. All 12,000 tickets for the show sold out in a record six hours. The 20-date tour of eight European countries was the first to feature auxiliary musicians on stage with the Stones, namely Bobby Keys on sax and Jim Price on trumpet. For the 1971 UK tour, Nicky Hopkins was added on piano alongside Ian 'Stu' Stewart.

...DIO TIME – 1972

...*xile On Main Street* largely recorded
...e summer of 1971 in the basement
... Nellcote, Keith's home on the
... Cote d'Azur, further work was
...ompleting and mixing the album at
... of the year in Los Angeles' Sunset
... Studios (where these Jim Marshall
...s were taken) which lasted into the
...ar. Many regard *Exile* as Keith's
...but as Richards pointed out: "The
...Mick spent most of his time during
...way, cause [wife] Bianca was
...nt; y'know, royalty is having a baby.
...t am I supposed to do? I'm
...ed to be making an album. But I
...onsidered it my album."

EXCESS ALL AREAS

The Rolling Stones' American Tour 1972 was the ultimate example of "if it's worth doing, it's worth doing to excess" – a maxim eloquently confirmed by Robert Frank's notorious film record of the tour, *Cocksucker Blues*, which remains unreleased. "The whole entourage had exploded in terms of numbers, of roadies and technicians, and of hangers-on and groupies," Richards wrote in his autobiography *Life* (Little, Brown 2010). "For the first time, we travelled in our own hired plane, with the lapping tongue painted on. We had become a pirate nation, moving on a huge scale under our own flag, with lawyers, clowns, attendants."

1973

The Stones started the year with a benefit show at the LA Forum for the Nicaraguan earthquake relief fund, then shows in Hawaii before arriving in Australia for a three-week tour. Keith can be seen playing his custom-made five-string guitar. "My usual rap about the five-string tuning – open G tuning – is that you need five strings, you get three notes, you use two fingers, and you get one arsehole to play it. But to me it rejuvenated my enthusiasm for playing guitar, because you'd put your fingers where you thought they'd go and you'd get accidents happening, and you wouldn't've done on regular tuning, because you'd know it too well."

BUSTED! AGAIN
....
A harried-looking Keith and Anita
arrive at Marlborough Street
Magistrates Court on June 27, 1973, to
answer drug and firearm charges,
where not guilty pleas were entered.
Four months later, the judge accepted
the defence's evidence and Keith was
fined £125 on firearm charges and £80
on the drugs charges. It was yet
another example of Richards' brushes
with the law over substances and by no
means the last. Later that evening, in a
stupor, Keith and Anita set fire to their
suite at the Londonderry House Hotel
and the Stones received a ban from
ever staying there again.

THE AFTERMATH OF THE REDLANDS ESTATE FIRE

Keith and flames went together that year of 1973 when Redlands' thatched roof caught fire during the night of July 31st, causing considerable damage before the local fire brigade brought it under control. To say that he and Anita were living their lives in a cavalier fashion was putting it mildly; not only were their activities a danger to themselves but also their young children

Marlon (nearly four) and 14-month-old daughter Dandelion. As Bill Wyman pointed out, the authorities tended to tar the other Stones with the same brush so they were in liable to receive the same treatment. Keith takes a well-earned cigarette break in an antique push chair (left) after a busy time salvaging belongings from the house (above).

FATHER'S LITTLE HELPER

Keith and Marlon together onstage during a soundcheck at the Wembley Empire Pool, London, September 7, 1973, on the Stones' European tour. Looking back on this time, Keith said: "My kids are the straightest in the world… [Marlon] took care of me when I was doing heroin on the road… He's seen everything. To him it's not a big deal. It's just something dad did."

I've known Ronnie stoned out of his brain, and I've known him straight sober. Quite honestly, there's very little difference.

THE CAT IN THE HAT – ROLLING STONES TOUR OF THE AMERICAS – 1975

With Mick Taylor's sudden decision to leave The Rolling Stones in December 1974, the band spent much of the early part of 1975 casting around for a replacement guitarist while recording their next album *Black And Blue*. Ronnie Wood was still part of The Faces when Jagger approached him to be "on loan" for the Stones' gargantuan 1975 Tour Of The Americas. 'Woody' was also the natural choice for Keith. "I love to play lead [guitar], but I like to sneak in, which is why I love to play with Ronnie [Wood]. With a quick nod and a wink, we can switch over in what we call the ancient art of weaving." The pair hit it off from the moment they properly met in 1973. To escape the attentions of the Chelsea Drug Squad, Keith even lived for a time in the cottage at the bottom of the garden at The Wick, Ronnie's estate on Richmond Hill.

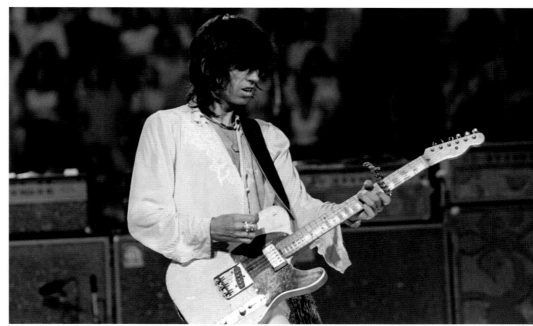

PRETTY BEAT UP

Keith in Brussels, May 1976, at a time when his condition was arguably at its worst. A fortnight later, driving back from a Stones gig in Stafford, he fell asleep at the wheel of his Bentley on the M1 near Newport Pagnell and crashed through a barrier, ending up in a field. Police charged him on suspicion of being in possession of drugs as a result. In June tragedy struck when he and Anita's baby son Tara died of a flu virus. But by far the most serious incident occurred in February 1977 when the couple were busted in Toronto. As well as heroin possession, Richards faced a trafficking charge which carried with it a minimum seven-year sentence.

"I was asleep when I got busted… I had been at rehearsal, got back to the hotel and passed out. My next memory is being woken up and dragged around by these two very big people who were slapping me awake… Canada was the crunch. The shit hit the fan big time."

SING ME BACK HOME

In the midst of all this personal drama,
there were less turbulent moments as
demonstrated by these and the following
pictures (pages 110-111) taken at Keith's
home in Connecticut, Massachusetts.

Playing live with the Stones is like living in your own separate country. It's like having an empire but no land.

THE TWO AMIGOS

In October 1978, a Toronto judge ruled that Keith would be better off propping up bars than doing time behind them and imposed a one-year suspended sentence after the court concluded that Richards did not import the heroin, but purchased it while in Canada. Keith credited the help of a diehard blind Stones fan, whom he looked out for when she attended Stones' shows, for saving his bacon: "This chick went to the judge's house in Toronto, personally, and she told him this simple story, y'know? And from there I think he figured out the best way to get Canada and himself and myself off of the hook. And so I was sentenced to a concert for the blind which I gladly performed. And my blind angel came through, bless her heart." The two charity concerts for The Canadian National Institute for the Blind took place at Oshawa Civic Auditorium on April 22, 1979 with the Stones' headlining set preceded by the baptism of The New Barbarians, Ronnie Wood's side project featuring Keith, former Face Ian McLagan on keyboards, Bobby Keys (sax), Stanley Clarke (bass) and drummer Ziggy Modeliste (from The Meters). These pics (and those on page 116) were taken during the Barbarians' American tour that followed.

A SALUTE TO JERRY LEE

Keith wearing a tuxedo "for the first time in my life" in a Salute to Jerry Lee Lewis, Los Angeles, July 16, 1983. Like Keith, Jerry Lee had frequently outwitted the Grim Reaper with his wildfire behaviour. Although in their early blues phase he and Mick were often dismissive of many of the fifties rock 'n' rollers, in later years, Keith's admiration knew no bounds. "Chills and fever down my left side" was his description of first hearing 'the Killer' and, in 2006, Richards was one of the distinguished musical guests appearing on Jerry Lee's album *Last Man Standing*.

I GOT THE BLUES

Keith hanging out at Rolling Stones Records' office in New York, 1980. Having kept off the hard stuff for the best part of three years, and his frequently destructive relationship with Anita Pallenberg at an end, Richards was now ready to take a more functional role in running the band but this seemed to not go down well with Mick. "When I cleaned up and *Emotional Rescue* time came around, I told Mick, 'Hey, I'm back, I'm clean, I'm ready; I'm back to help and take some weight off your shoulders' – immediately I got a sense of resentment. Whereas I felt that he would be happy to unburden himself of some of that shit, he felt that I was homing in and trying to take control. And that's when I first sensed the feeling of discontent, shall we say."

MR & MRS RICHARDS

On his 40th birthday, December 18, 1983, Keith and girlfriend Patti Hansen tied the knot at the Finisterra Hotel in Cabo San Lucas, Mexico, in front of close friends and family including Keith's parents who had separated when he was young. Mick was best man and at the reception afterwards Keith serenaded the new Mrs Richards with an impromptu version of Hoagy Carmichael's 'The Nearness Of You'.

THREE OF A KIND

Eric Clapton, Chuck Berry and Keith at Chuck's Los Angeles home during the filming of Taylor Hackford's documentary *Hail! Hail! Rock 'n' Roll*, 1986. The great rock 'n' roller, celebrating his 60th birthday, was feted in a celebratory concert organised by Keith in St Louis, Berry's birthplace. "One of the reasons I worked with Chuck Berry was that I felt I owed him so much. When I started I pinched virtually all of his riffs, you know? But I figure I repaid my debt because he was one of the most difficult persons I've ever worked with apart from Mick Jagger... I thought if I turned this down I'll have to live with the fact that I chickened out. Because when I started to play the electric guitar, Chuck Berry was my man."

The wife's always asking, "why are you lighting up another cigarette?" I tell her it's because the last one wasn't long enough.

JOHN LEE HOOKER

Keith with another of his heroes, venerable bluesman John Lee Hooker. "Most of the people I've ever wanted to play with, I've played with. When I started playing guitar the idea of playing with Muddy Waters was 'when I get to heaven… if I make it there and he makes it there…' But I actually got to play with him, John Lee, Howlin' Wolf, Scotty Moore, in a small room, asking him 'How the hell did you do that?'… I actually got to play with them all. You can't ask much more than that from life. And I got paid!"

TALK IS CHEAP

Keith in a 1988 photo session promoting his first solo album *Talk Is Cheap*. Of all the Stones, Keith was most loathe to step outside the Stones' circle, feeling it was a form of admission that he couldn't cut it with his main band. However, with his professional and personal relationship with Mick Jagger at an all-time low, Richards gathered together a bunch of musicians he dubbed The X-Pensive Winos and hit the road in support of an album that was an unexpected delight. "We recorded the whole thing basically like we would with the Stones with everyone playing live in the studio which apparently now is a novelty. I don't know why. To me that's one of the most essential things about making a rock 'n' roll record. It has to be spontaneous with lots of room-sound, ambience. Let the sound buzz around the room instead of tightening it up and keeping everyone sounding clear and clean and in a box."

I've never had a problem with drugs, only with policemen.

THE ROAD TO STEEL WHEELS

Keith in front of Neal Preston's camera, 1988. Many of the interviews he gave at this time, ostensibly to promote *Talk Is Cheap*, were thinly veiled attacks on his erstwhile singer, then busy promoting his own solo works. Despite a printed warning from Richards that "if he tours without the band, I'll slit his throat!" Mick played solo shows in Japan and Australia. A process of appeasement, instigated by Ronnie Wood, eventually lead to the two meeting in Barbados to collaborate on what became the Stones' "comeback" album *Steel Wheels* in 1989.

STEEL WHEELS

On August 12, the Stones performed an unannounced warm-up club show at Toad's Place, in New Haven, Connecticut – the first time they had been on stage together for three-and-a-half years. The tour itself kicked off on August 31 at Veteran's Stadium, Philadelphia. As seen here (and on pages 137-138), Keith was plainly delighted to be back on the road with 'his' band, and unlike the seventies Stones' tours, he was in a better state to appreciate things. "The heavy drugs are out, of course. I'd be an idiot – probably wouldn't be here – if I hadn't cut them out. But I don't look to go through life being someone's image of Keith Richards. I'm inside him. The idea of partying for nine days in order to keep the image of Keith Richards is stupid. That was Keith Richards then. Now I'll stay up just two or three days."

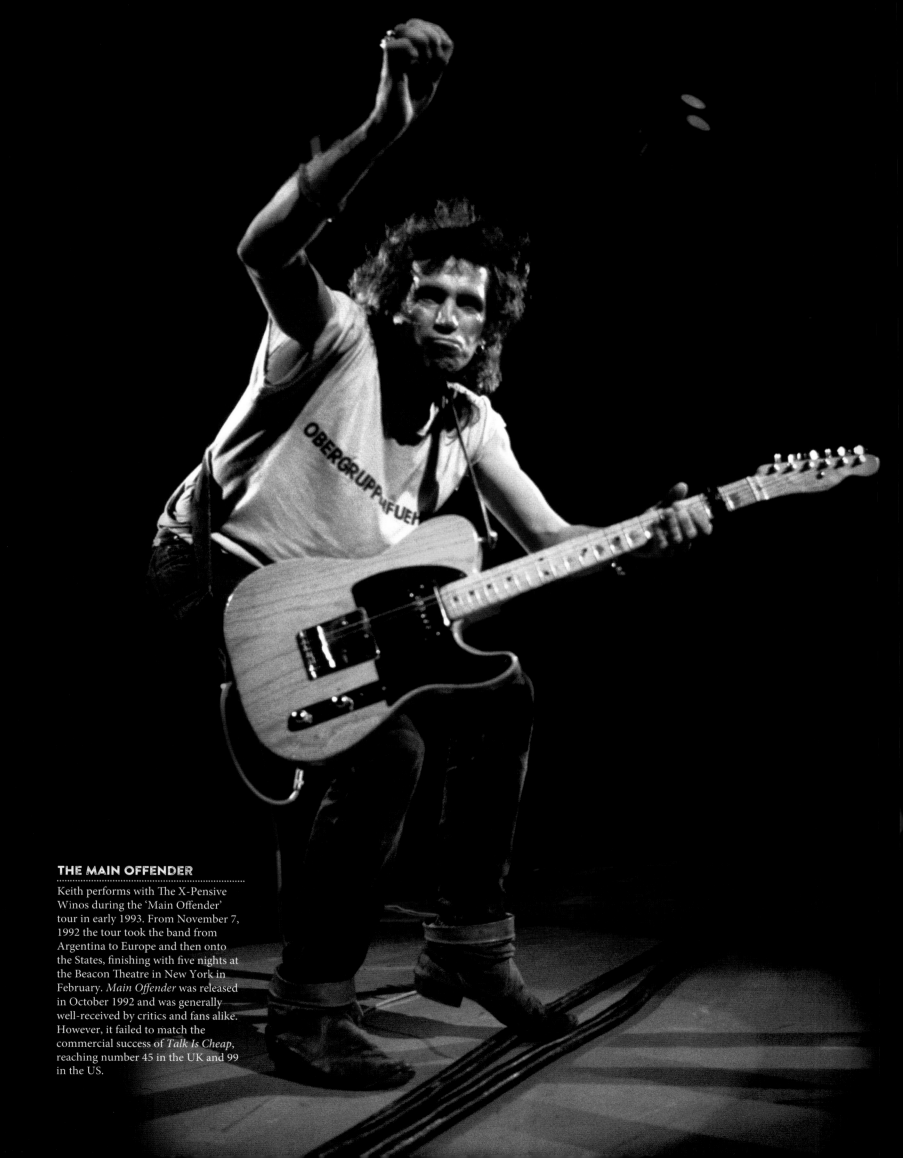

THE MAIN OFFENDER

Keith performs with The X-Pensive
Winos during the 'Main Offender'
tour in early 1993. From November 7,
1992 the tour took the band from
Argentina to Europe and then onto
the States, finishing with five nights at
the Beacon Theatre in New York in
February. *Main Offender* was released
in October 1992 and was generally
well-received by critics and fans alike.
However, it failed to match the
commercial success of *Talk Is Cheap*,
reaching number 45 in the UK and 99
in the US.

VOODOO LOUNGE

Starting out on August 1, 1994 in Washington DC, the Voodoo Lounge Tour was the first Stones trek without Bill Wyman who announced his 'retirement' in 1991. Keith was livid. "If we did go on tour without Bill, I'm sure he'll be very pissed off and that's what I'm counting on. But then, Bill's from a different generation. For him, success is going on *The Michael Aspel Show*. I think he's on his third menopause; certainly can't be his first." Wyman was replaced, though not as a full member, by session bassist Darryl Jones.

VOODOO LOUNGE HITS EUROPE

The fourth and final leg of the Voodoo Lounge Tour saw the Stones return to Europe for 39 shows that began in Amsterdam and ended in Rotterdam on August 30. Here's Keith tearing up the Goffertpark in Nijmegen on June 13, 1995. The tour, over four legs with 129 shows, grossed $320 million, becoming the highest grossing tour of any artist at that time. In the midst of all this professional efficiency, Mick and Keith's working relationship was still respectfully distant. "Though Keith is more sensitive then I, we didn't have any major rows," said Jagger of their rift in the eighties. "We're not an old married couple who can't live together and can't live apart; we're two men who've been friends for 30 years. Occasionally you want to strangle even the closest of friends."

BRIDGES TO BABYLON TOUR

The Bridges to Babylon Tour was the second largest grossing tour at the time, behind the Stones' own record-breaking 1994–1995 Voodoo Lounge Tour. It was believed 4,577,000 people attended over the 108 shows: 2,020,000 in Europe, 2,009,000 in North America, 348,000 in Argentina and Brazil, and 200,000 in Japan. The tour reached 25 countries and is the second largest North American tour of all time – second to the 2005–2007 A Bigger Bang Tour. It was also the first tour where a smaller 'B-stage' in the middle of the arena was featured at most shows. The band would stride across the bridge from the main stage and play several numbers there. Asked what his favourite Richards' riff was, Keith replied, "My favourite Keef riff? I play it all the time! Every one's the same, it's a variation on the same old thing!"

HOME

Keith with foot on the keys at home in Westchester, Connecticut. Even a quiet place for reflection such as this could not escape the 'Keef factor'. On the eve of the Stones' European tour in 1998, Keith stood precariously on a chair in his library to reach a book about Leonardo da Vinci's study of anatomy when he slipped, bringing several heavy tomes down on top of him. The accident resulted in three broken ribs for Keith and a tour postponement for the Stones. "It was one of those moments where you have to make a decision: take it in the ribs or take a shot in the temple on the desk. All part of life's rich pageant."

THE CONCERT FOR NEW YORK CITY

The Concert for New York City was a benefit staged at Madison Square Garden on October 20, 2001 in response to the September 11 attacks. Organised by Paul McCartney, the event featured many famous musical names including The Who, Eric Clapton, David Bowie, and Elton John. The Stones were in hiatus at the time but Mick and Keith rallied to perform 'Salt Of The Earth' and 'Miss You'.

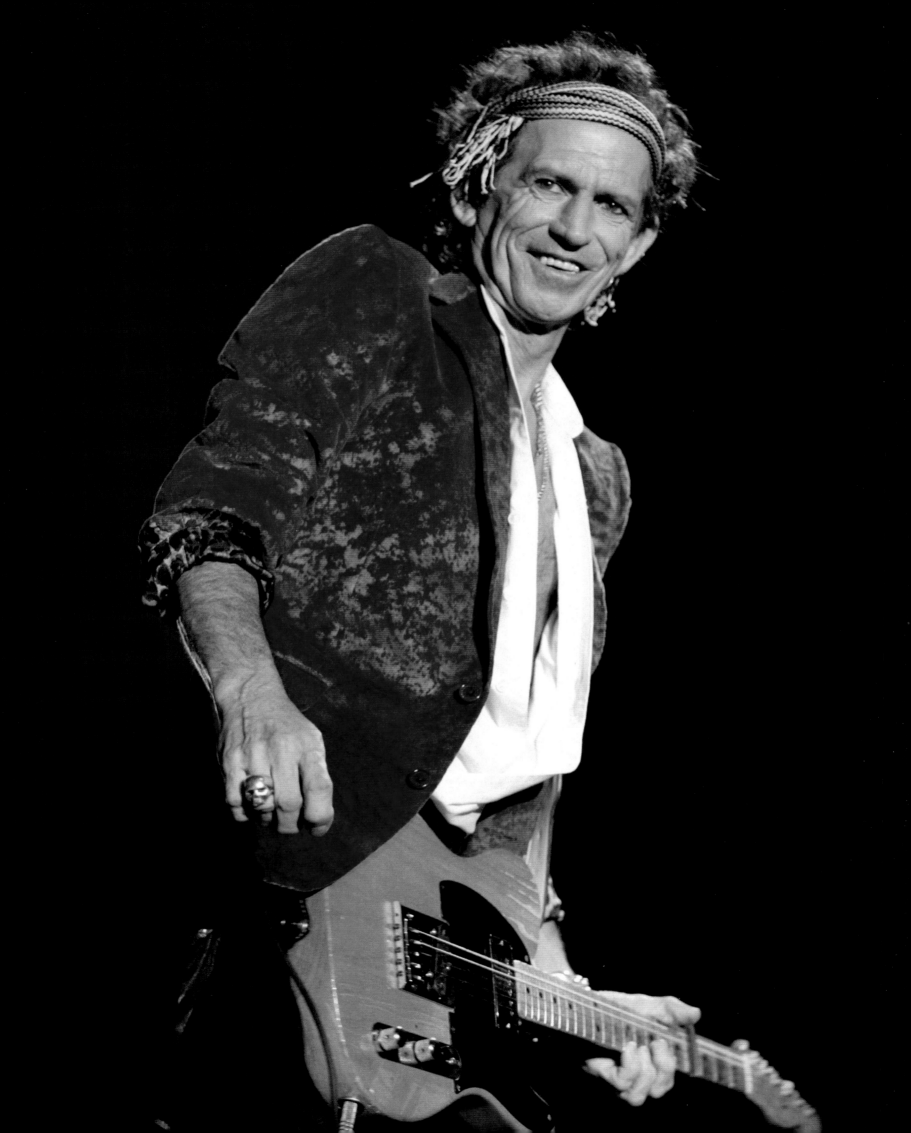

FORTY LICKS

The Stones turned 40 in 2002, starting yet another lucrative world tour. At nearly 60, Keith, especially, was not ready to hang up his rock 'n' roll boots. "Nobody ever turned around to Muddy Waters, BB King or John Lee Hooker and said 'Now you have to stop; you're not allowed to play any longer.'

I played with Muddy just six months before he died and I'd never heard him play better – still powerful because he knew how best to conserve his energies in a different way. This was a man at the tail end of his life, yet still able to perform with such creativity."

THE ARMOURY

An artist has many brushes and Keith has many guitars to deliver the distinctive Stones sound. 'Malcolm' is a 1954 Fender Telecaster with natural finish. 'Sonny' is a 1966 Fender Telecaster Sunburst. 'Dice' is a 1957 Gibson Les Paul TV Model Yellow. 'Dwight' is a White 1964 Gibson ES-345 Stereo. And the guitar prominent in this shot is his 1959 Black Gibson ES-355 Mono. 'Micawber', probably his most famous trademark guitar, is a 1953 Fender Telecaster Blonde. "There's no reason for my guitar being called Micawber apart from the fact that it's such an unlikely name. There's no-one around me called Micawber, so when I scream for Micawber everybody knows what

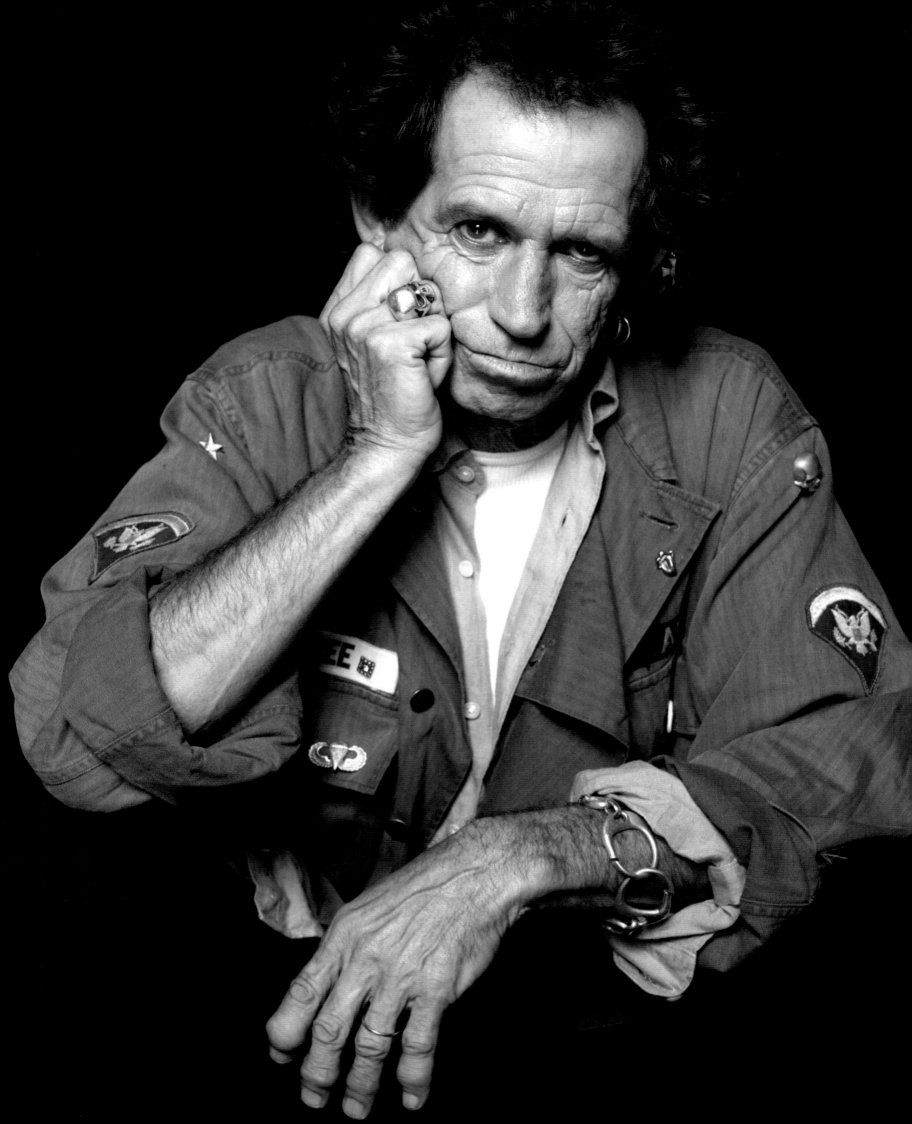

Some things get
better with age.
Like me.

LICKS TOUR

Another stage in another town – in this case the Olympic Stadium, Munich, Germany, June 6, 2003. "You can't whitewash the Stones. None of us minds the bread, but there's absolutely no way you could get Charlie Watts or, for that matter, any of us out there for the bread alone… Everyone in the Stones still loves the music they're playing and, individually, still don't think they're good enough as musicians. But we're still trying to better ourselves. Now, whether we actually achieve it or not is always open to debate. But if we retain this genuine enthusiasm, then maybe we can go on and face the future with a brave face."

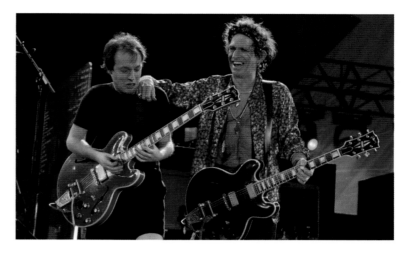

SARSFEST – TORONTO, ONTARIO, CANADA ON JULY 30, 2003

Officially titled Molson Canadian Rocks for Toronto, but commonly referred to as SARSfest, this show was a benefit to help Toronto's struggling economy and once-thriving tourism industry, which was savaged by the severe acute respiratory syndrome (SARS) outbreak accompanied by a travel warning issued by the World Health Organization. The benefit was organized at the behest of the Stones, who wanted to help the city they have had a long – and sometimes sordid – connection to. "I have a strange relationship with this town," as Keith put it mildly. Other artists on the bill included The Guess Who, Rush and AC/DC – Angus Young (top right) along with his brother Malcolm guested on 'Rock Me Baby' during the Stones' set.

BANG! AND THEY'RE OFF

The A Bigger Bang World Tour World Tour began with a surprise performance on May 10, 2005 at the Julliard Music School Plaza in New York City. Mick and Keith's working association was put to the test after Jagger became 'Sir Mick' in December 2003. Richards declared he could not share a stage with someone wearing a "coronet and sporting the old ermine" and told Jagger it was a "paltry honour". "I thought it was ludicrous to take one of those gongs from the establishment," Keith railed, "when they did their very best to throw us in jail." Relations were to get even more glacial in 2010 with the raw opinions contained in Richards' autobiography, particularly Keith's flippant comments about the size of Mick's manhood, something the world's tabloids gleefully seized upon.

SHINE A LIGHT

For years, director and über-fan Martin Scorsese had used Rolling Stones music effectively in film classics like *Mean Streets* and *Goodfellas* so it seemed inevitable that the two would eventually meet in some form of celluloid collaboration. Scorsese's team filmed the Stones at the Beacon Theatre, NYC on October 29 and November 1, 2006, but the performance footage used in *Shine A Light* is all from the second show. The music was recorded, mixed and co-produced by Stones' associate Bob Clearmountain. The concert footage is preceded by a brief semi-fictionalised introduction about the preparations for the shows, including a rather nauseating meet and greet backstage with the Clintons, and intercut with historical news clips and archival interviews with band members.

PIRATE LORD OF MADAGASCAR

In 2007 Keith Richards joined the
Pirates Of The Caribbean franchise as
Edward Teague, Pirate Lord of
Madagascar. He was a natural choice
for the role of Jack Sparrow's father
since Johnny Depp, a long-time fan,
had partially modelled his lead
character on the legendary guitarist.
Asked whether he saw any similarity
between the roles of rock star and pirate
lord, Richards said: "Actually, you
could look at it like that. Both are ways
to make a good dishonest living."

ISLE OF WIGHT FESTIVAL

Almost 40 years since Keith watched Dylan on the offshore island, the Stones played their own headlining set at the revived festival there in front of 60,000 people on June 10, 2007. It was also the Stones' first British festival performance for over 30 years, since their appearance at the 1976 Knebworth Fair. The set-list featured special guests in the form of Paolo Nutini (who sang on 'Love In Vain') and Amy Winehouse (on 'Ain't Too Proud To Beg'). Keith was growing a moustache for his role in the *Pirates Of The Carribean* series.

POSTER BOY

At 64, Keith became the face of Louis Vuitton, the French fashion house whose name is synonymous with luxury handbags, luggage and, just for Keith, guitar cases. His image appeared on a billboard outside the brand's New Bond Street flagship store in London and in an international advertising operation, created by Ogilvy & Mather, which appeared in British newspapers in March 2008. Keith joined the likes of former Soviet leader Mikhail Gorbachev and actress Catherine Deneuve in the campaign which was brought to life by the celebrated American portrait photographer Annie Leibovitz, who had earned her stripes as the concert tour photographer for The Rolling Stones Tour of the Americas '75.

THAT'S LIFE

With more than a lifetime of tales, it was time to put pen to paper and unleash the memoir. Published in October 2010, *Life* told Keith's incredible story from his childhood in Dartford, through to his success with The Rolling Stones and his current life in Connecticut. Keith poses with *Life* at the New York Public Library on October 29, 2010 (opposite) and at a signing session at Waterstone's Booksellers, London on November 3, 2010 (above). The book debuted, and spent two weeks, at the top position on The *New York Times* hardback non-fiction best-sellers' list and went on to receive the 2011 Norman Mailer Prize for biography. Richards was also named Writer of the Year at the *GQ* Men of the Year awards.

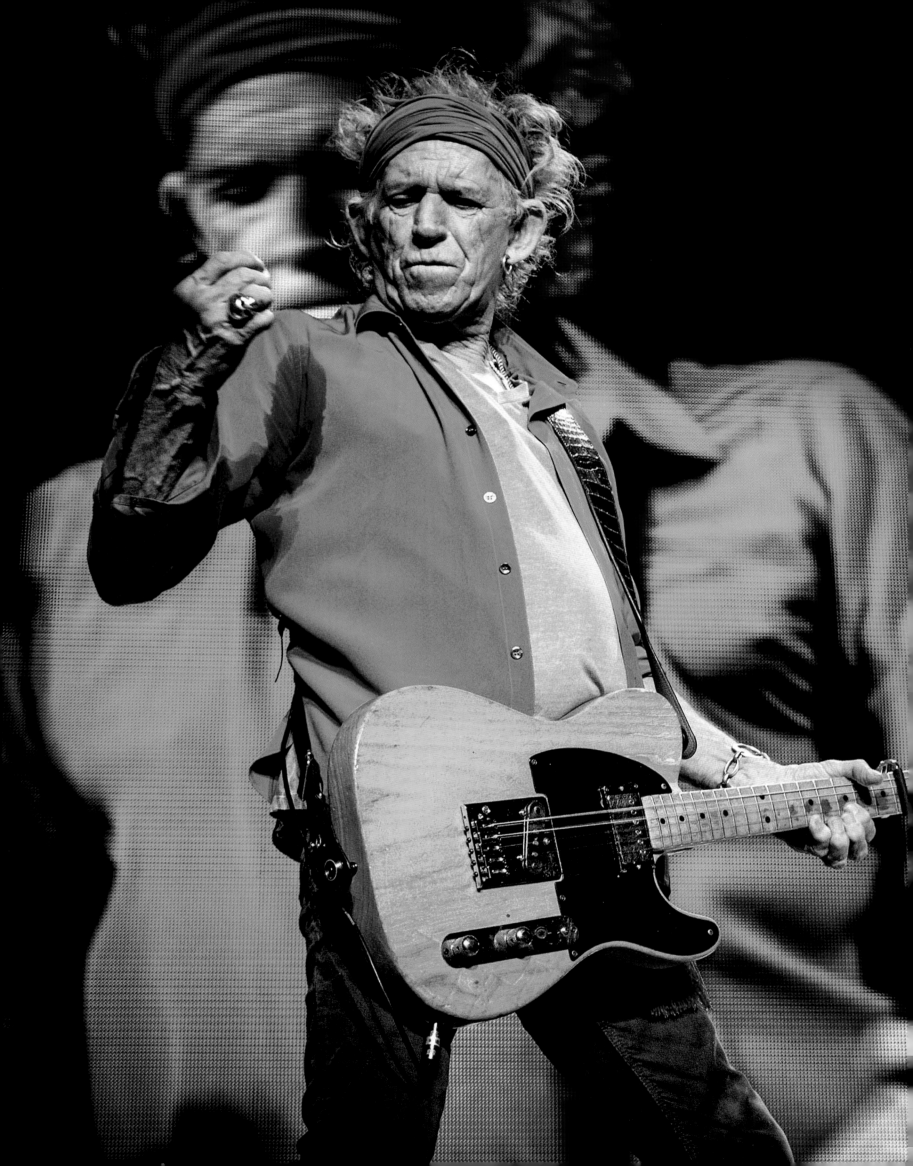

Micawber is a '53.
and I have a '54 Tele
named Malcolm.
They always start
with M....

GLASTONBURY

On the eve of the Stones' highly-anticipated appearance at the Glastonbury Festival on June 29, 2013, Keith admitted to some nerves. "I think the only pressure we feel is that it is the first time we've done an outdoor show for yonks and the English weather. Throwing in those two equations, yeah, there is maybe a little apprehension."

He also proffered an explanation as to why the Stones had never played Glastonbury before. "It just never occurred. Many times it has been on the list of tours and stuff and for one reason or another it never coincided. It's like a black hole in space or something but in we go this time. I'm looking forward to it because it is an iconic

gig and it's an iconic band [so] finally the two meet at last. In a way it's kind of weird that at last we've made it to Glastonbury. It's like building Stonehenge right?" Michael Eavis, founder of the annual festival, later described the Stones' appearance on the Pyramid Stage in front of over 100,000 revellers as "the high spot of 43 years".

It's almost as if we were finally destined to play Glastonbury.

CHINA

Keith on stage at the Cotai Arena, Beijing, March 9, 2014 during the 14 On Fire Tour. It was the Stones' second visit, having first played China in 2006. The band had originally been due to tour there in 2003 but the gigs were cancelled due to the SARS crisis. In 2006, the bad boys of rock who kowtowed to no one were forced to bow to government censorship after submitting their lyrics to Chinese authorities for vetting (as all western bands had to do), and drop certain songs like 'Brown Sugar', 'Honky Tonk Women' and 'Let's Spend The Night Together' from the set-list. For this tour, Mick Taylor was a welcome re-addition, although he was used only sparingly on 'Midnight Rambler', 'Satisfaction' and Keith's 'Slipping Away'.

THE ROCK STAR. THE REBEL. THE PIRATE. THE CHILDREN'S AUTHOR.

In 2014, having become a grandfather for the fifth time, Keith decided to add children's author to his considerable CV with the release of *Gus & Me: The Story Of My Grandad And My First Guitar*. It tells the story of Keith's beloved granddad, Theodore Augustus Dupree, affectionately known as "Gus", who was in a jazz big band. Gus introduced his grandson to the joy of music and gave him his first guitar. The rest as they say, is history. The book features illustrations by Keith's daughter, Theodora Dupree Richards, who is named after the man that was so special in Keith's childhood. Keith and Theodora backstage at *The Tonight Show Starring Jimmy Fallon* at NBC Studios on September 9, 2014, in New York City while promoting the book.

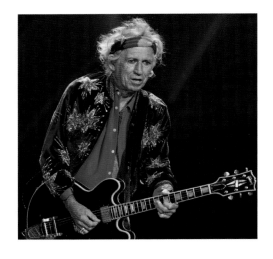

14 ON FIRE

Keith and the Stones on fire in Melbourne, November 5, 2014. "I'm not a kid any more, and I've thought to myself how long can I keep doing this? That's the great thing about it – the not-knowing. But within the narrow confines of rock 'n' roll, it's for me to find out how to use my experience and produce something that hopefully is still worth listening to. Like I said, somebody has got to find out how far you can take this thing, and I guess it might just as well be me."

ZIP CODE TOUR

The Stones just keep on rolling. On May 24, 2015, it was announced that the band would be treading the boards again with the summer Zip Code Tour. Opening in San Diego, the 15-city sweep is scheduled to conclude in Quebec City, Canada on July 15. "We love being out on the road and it is great to come back to North America," Keith said via a press release, adding with characteristic understatement, "I can't wait to get back on the stage!"

.After all is said and done I did alright, I had my fun...

PHOTO CREDITS

Cover photo by John Stoddart/Getty Images

Photographs supplied by:

© Jay Blakesberg, © Michael Cooper Collection, © Deborah Feingold/Corbis, © Getty Images,
© Dezo Hoffman/Rex Features/Shutterstock, © Jim Marshall Photography LLC, Gered Mankowitz
© Bowstir 2015, © Mirrorpix, © Paul Natkin/Getty Images, © Terry O'Neill/Getty Images,
© Scarlet Page, © Jan Persson/Getty Images, © Neal Preston, © Michael Putland/Getty Images,
© Steve Pyke/Getty Images, © Ken Regan/Camera 5/Contour by Getty Images,
© Rex Features/Shutterstock, © Ebet Roberts/Getty Images, © Christopher Simon Sykes/Getty
Images, © Philip Townshend/Camera Press

All photographs used with permission of the copyright holder.